Hi, I'r

D1413035

And your name is...? _ _ _ _ _ _ _ _ _ _ _ _ _ _ _ _ _ _ _

It's Called Dyslexia

Jennifer Moore-Mallinos
Illustrations: Marta Fàbrega

THE O'BRIEN PRESS
DUBLIN

This book has been published by
The O'Brien Press
and
the Dyslexia Association of Ireland
with the support of
Hasbro's National Game Playing Week.

For further information on dyslexia in Ireland, please contact:

Dyslexia Association of Ireland,
Suffolk Chambers,
1 Suffolk Street,
Dublin 2.
www.dyslexia.ie

LEARNING HOW TO READ AND WRITE

This year at school I'm going to
learn how to read and write.
It's going to be so much fun!
There are so many books I want
to explore, especially the ones
about dinosaurs.

So far, I can make all the sounds
of the letters in the alphabet, but
sometimes I still have trouble putting
the sounds together and figuring out
a word. I get all mixed up! Whenever
this happens, I get mad and I just
want to give up. But then I think
about all those dinosaur books
I want to read, and I keep trying.

IT'S VERY CONFUSING!

I FEEL SAD

As each day goes by, I'm still having trouble reading.
Sometimes I feel so sad that I pretend I'm sick just
so I don't have to go to school. Why can't I be like
the other kids? Why can't I read?

I TRY HARD ON ALL MY WORK

I like going to school and seeing my friends, and I try really hard on all my work, so yesterday when my teacher stopped at my desk and asked to speak to me, I was scared. She said she was worried about my work and that she wanted to meet with Mom and Dad to talk to them. Now I don't know how to feel!

WHY CAN'T I READ AND WRITE WELL?

The next day during the meeting with my teacher, Mom and Dad found out I was having a lot of trouble with my reading and writing. My teacher said she wanted me to do some special tests so she would know how to help me. Maybe there was a reason why I had so much trouble learning to read and write.

I HAVE DYSLEXIA, BUT
I'LL IMPROVE

A few days after I finished taking all the tests, I found out I had DYSLEXIA. People with dyslexia have trouble understanding the sounds within words, which makes it difficult to learn how to read. Often they have problems understanding what they hear, like following directions, putting things in the right order, or remembering how to put sounds and words together to make words. They also get confused with the directions of letters like "b" and "d" or even reverse words like "tip" and "pit." Some people with dyslexia also have difficulty with handwriting and trying to write down their thoughts. Dyslexia can't be cured, but it can get better with a lot of help and practice.

A LITTLE HELP AND LOTS OF WORK

At first I was scared, but my teacher explained that having dyslexia just meant that it would take me longer to learn how to read and write. It didn't mean I wasn't smart, and it didn't mean that I couldn't be good at other things. It meant that with extra help and hard work I could learn how to listen, read, and write without so much difficulty.

PLENTY OF HELP AT SCHOOL AND AT HOME

Ever since I found out I have dyslexia, I've been getting extra help at school and in my home. At school I'm in a special class with other kids who have problems just like me. The teacher uses special programs to improve our listening, reading, and writing skills. At home, Mom and Dad are doing many fun activities with me, and I am getting good results.

MY READING IS IMPROVING

It took so much practice and hard work, but my reading's getting better, and I don't feel so sad anymore. I don't even remember the last time I pretended to be sick. And those dinosaur books I always wanted to read are even better than I thought they'd be! My teacher is showing us all kinds of tricks for remembering and paying attention, so that learning gets easier.

POETRY IS AWESOME!

Today my teacher read some poems to the class. I didn't know poetry could be so neat and I loved it! I liked it so much that when the teacher asked us to make our very own book of poems, I was excited! I couldn't wait to show the teacher all the poems I was going to write, especially now that I could write better.

IT'S NOT AS CONFUSING AS IT USED TO BE

Even though I had to use my dictionary to spell many of the words in my poems, I didn't get as confused as I did before. I didn't want to give up either. It took me a few days to write all of my poems but I had so much fun doing it! It's so helpful when I use the computer to write! I don't have to worry about my handwriting, and it's easier to correct mistakes like spelling.

When I began school, I'd get very scared to read in front of the class. Sometimes I was so scared that I'd hide behind the person in front of me and hope that the teacher wouldn't pick me to read. But not anymore! I couldn't wait to read my poems to the class, and I wasn't as worried about making mistakes either.

I READ IN FRONT OF
THE ENTIRE CLASS!

I HAVE A SPECIAL TALENT

After I read a couple of my poems to my class, everyone stood up and clapped. They really liked them! My teacher said that I had a special talent for writing poetry, and that she couldn't wait to read the rest of my poems in my poem book.

I HAVE DYSLEXIA, AND THAT'S OK

I have dyslexia, but I can live with it. I have to work harder and practice longer so I can learn how to read and write, but it's worth it! I feel so much better about myself, especially now that I learned I have a special talent! Maybe one day I'll be famous like Albert Einstein, Leonardo da Vinci, Walt Disney, Beethoven, and even movie stars like Tom Cruise and Whoopie Goldberg! They all had dyslexia, too!

Activities

FLASH CARDS

Flash cards are a great way to help you learn new words and to remember words you already know.

Items needed:
Cardboard or construction paper, scissors, markers, dictionary.
Art supplies, such as colored pencils, crayons, glue, glitter glue, and so on.

How to make flash cards:
1. Cut several pieces of cardboard or construction paper into the same size shape, approximately 2 inches by 3 inches.
2. Using a marker or crayon, neatly print a word on one side of each of the cards. You may want to use a dictionary to make sure that you spell the word correctly.
3. If you can, draw a picture of the word on the other side to help you if you get stuck.
4. Be creative and decorate your flash cards. Use fancy designs, glitter glue and lots of color to make your cards "flashy!" (But don't overdo it: the word you wrote must stand out.)

Flash cards can be used by yourself, with a friend, or a parent. It's a great way to practice reading words, improve your memory, and have fun at the same time! Look at every card and memorize the names. Then try to write them all on a piece of paper. Then compare what you wrote with what is written on the cards. Are the words the same?

Once you master the words on your first set of flash cards, you may want to add more flash cards to your collection. Start your collection with words that are not as difficult. As you learn these words, create more flash cards with words that increase in their level of difficulty. By adding more cards, you will also improve your memory skills when you play the memory game!

MEMORY GAME

Make the flash cards as shown above, but now you will have to make a match for every flash card. For example, if one of the flash cards is the word "frog," you will need to make sure you have another flash card that also says "frog."

To play the game:
1. Lay several flash cards face down.
2. Turn over two cards at a time to try to find the match for each word.
3. If you don't find a match, flip the cards over and try again by turning over two more cards.
4. The object of the game is to find as many matches as you can in the least amount of turns. The one with the most matches wins!

Good luck and have fun.

PICTURE DICTIONARY

Everybody knows how useful a dictionary can be!
So let's make our very own dictionary that will always be helpful to us, at school and at home!

Items needed:
Construction paper, markers, crayons, pencils.
Art supplies: glue, glitter glue.
Three-hole punch, yarn, ruler, tabs or dividers.

1. Using approximately 28 pages of construction paper, punch three holes, evenly spaced along the left side of each page.
2. Cut three pieces of yarn (approximately 7 inches in length).
3. String and tie a piece of yarn through each of the holes. This will hold your book together.
4. Use tabs or dividers to label each new letter page. This will make it easier for you to locate a word when you use your dictionary.

Start your dictionary with words that you use often in your everyday writing. These words are called high-frequency words.

As you add words to your dictionary, draw a picture beside each word. If you like, write a definition as well.

Don't forget to create an interesting cover for your dictionary. Add as many pages as you like.

Be creative and have fun!

JUST FOR FUN...

Try ten new things and see which you like the most and which ones you do well. It can be a sport such as soccer, high jump, baseball, or running, or an activity such as dancing, singing, painting, writing, or learning photography or cooking.

Don't be shy, but be realistic. For example, for a child, sky-diving is not a realistic thing to want to try, but perhaps taking a guitar or karate class is!

How will you ever know if you are good at anything if don't give it a try? You'll feel so good about your efforts, just for the trying! What are you going to put on your list?

Ask for the help of an adult or parent to help you get started. Whether it's signing you up for a special class or activity or just giving you encouragement, I'm sure your parents will love to help you explore your talents!

Have fun and TRY!

Note to parents

All parents want their children to be successful. We want them to succeed in school, in life and to be happy. We want our children to grow up to be confident adults who can contribute and thrive within society in a meaningful way. Then, how do we as parents make this happen? What can we do to help our children to have a satisfying future? How do we help them to become successful learners?

The stepping-stones toward learning start with the most basic skills: reading, writing, and mathematics. These basic skills are the foundation on which knowledge is built. Therefore, there are high expectations placed on these primary skills for every child to master within a relatively short period of time. However, not all children will grasp these concepts as quickly as we would like, and some will require additional support to do so.

Children who struggle in any area of academics whether it's reading, writing, or math, often experience stress and frustration. This will ultimately develop into a reluctance to go to school as well as a display of negative behaviors, such as uncooperativeness, defiance, and even depression and withdrawal. These behaviors, in combination with poor achievement, may indicate an even greater problem that will require further exploration in order to identify the core issue.

A child who is having difficulty learning how to read and write or who is struggling to master certain skills will show a repeated pattern of mistakes.

Approximately 10 to 15 percent of the population are dyslexic, but many of these people are not identified in early childhood. Although there are almost an equal number of boys and girls affected, boys tend to show their symptoms much earlier than girls do.

The symptoms of dyslexia indicate a problem with auditory processing, that is, the ability to recognize, analyze, segment, and blend sounds. People affected often have difficulty processing and understanding what they hear, especially when attempting to learn the connection between letters and sounds. They may have problems comprehending rapid instructions or following more than one command at a time. Difficulty with reading emerges early on, when children fail to see and hear similarities and differences in letters and sounds and therefore can't assemble the parts of words.

One of the common signs of dyslexia is reversals. Reversals occur when a person confuses letters by either reading or writing letters incorrectly, such as "b" and "d," or when a word order is reversed, such as "rats" read as "star" or "not" read as "ton."

Subsequent spelling, writing, and handwriting difficulties often result. Mathematics skills may also be affected when a child can't remember math facts. The symptoms of dyslexia vary from individual to individual, but in-depth evaluation can highlight both strengths and weaknesses.

In the classroom, the struggle with decoding often makes it difficult for children to comprehend reading matter as well as to convey their thoughts on paper. As a result, they may feel frustrated, embarrassed, and discouraged, and do whatever they can to avoid reading and writing. In many cases, "bad" behavior will become the distraction or way out of having to address their difficulties.

Unfortunately, when children experience failure on a regular basis, they will also experience low self-esteem and sometimes describe themselves as "stupid." For this reason, it is very important that parents and educators attempt to increase a child's confidence level through consistent praise and support.

As mentioned in the story, it may also be beneficial to find an activity in which the child does well. This will help him or her with confidence and the positive feelings associated with success.

A child diagnosed with dyslexia does not lack intelligence, potential, or the ability to become a successful and confident member of society. In fact, there are many famous people who were diagnosed with dyslexia. Some had to struggle without special help and others learned to adapt to their diagnosis. Despite their difficulties, they were able to make valuable contributions to society.

Parents are the most important advocates for their children. Be aware, at all times, that specialized instruction, one-to-one tutorial, and plenty of determination and positive support will make the difference. Every child with dyslexia can be successful!

This edition published 2010 by The O'Brien Press Ltd,
12 Terenure Road East, Rathgar, Dublin 6, Ireland.
Tel: +353 1 4923333; Fax: +353 1 4922777
E-mail: books@obrien.ie
Website: www.obrien.ie
Reprinted 2010.

Original title of the book in English:
IT'S CALLED DYSLEXIA
(c) Copyright GEMSER PUBLICATIONS S.L.,
2,00XC/ Castell, 38; Teià (08329) Barcelona, Spain
(World Rights) Tel: 93 540 13 53,
E-mail: info@mercedesros.com
Website: www.mercedesros.com
Author: Jennifer Moore-Mallinos
Illustrator: Marta Fàbrega

ISBN: 978-1-84717-203-7

A catalogue record for this title is available
from the British Library.

2 3 4 5 6 7 8 9 10
10 11 12 13 14 15 16

Printed in China